BEYOND SALES
The Trilogy Approach to Growing Your Business

Copyright © 2011 by Trilogy Partners, LLC
All rights reserved

No part of this document may be reproduced in any form or by any electronic or mechanical means, including information storage and retrieval systems, without permission in writing from the authors.

The information presented herein represents the views of the authors as of the date of publication. This document is presented for informational purposes only. Due to the rate at which conditions change, the authors reserve the right to alter and update their opinions at any time. While every attempt has been made to verify the information in this document, the authors do not assume any responsibility for errors, inaccuracies or omissions.

Trilogy Partners, LLC
3967 Princeton Pike, Suite B
Princeton, NJ 08540
609-688-0428
http://www.gettrilogypartners.com

TABLE OF CONTENTS

Foreword 5
    Why Do I Need More Sales?   6
    Our Point of View   7

Introduction 9
    Is Sales Your Real Problem?   10
    We Just Need More Sales Leads   12

Who is the Right Customer? 15
    Who Is the *Right* Customer for Our Business?   16
    Does My Value Proposition Fit My *Right* Customer?   17
    Who Are My Actual Customers?   18
    Can I "Fire" My Wrong Customers?   19
    Have I Planned to Grow My Business with the Right Customers?   19
    Do I Have the Resources to Add New Customers?   20
    Do I Really Need New Customers?   21
    Are You Listening to Your Right Customers?   22

Choosing the Best Sales and Growth Strategies 23
    Client Retention   24
    Increasing Customer Spend   26
    Adding Products/Services to Meet Client Need   28
    Small Firms Can Compete with Large Firms and Win!   29

BEYOND SALES   Table of Contents

Growth through Niche and Micro-Niche Building	30
Principles of Micro-Niche Building	32

Planning for Growth   35

Customer Selection Process	36
Client Acquisition Process	37
Plan Components	37

About the Authors   39

Douglas S. Brown, CAIA, CBC, CDIA, CVIA	40
John Sheridan	40
David Wolfskehl	41
Hal Levenson, Founding Partner	42

About Trilogy Partners, LLC   43

FOREWORD

EVERYBODY KNOWS selling is about customers. You cannot make a sale without a customer. Without customers making purchases, you have shopping baskets sitting around empty. Without customers – especially new customers – the future of the company will look dismal.

This means we value customers. We know we cannot run a business without customers. We offer products and services customers will want to buy.

This might all be true. It does not mean, however, that you necessarily have a customer-focused sales strategy. Ask yourself if any of these statements are true about your company:

- Our *sales team* thinks selling is about them – their ability to sell what we give them.
- Our *customer service team* thinks everything is about them. They think answering questions and solving problems drives sales.
- Our *product/service development team* understands each sale as an indication of their success in understanding the market and providing products that will bring in customers.
- Our *marketing team* views sales as a direct outcome of the success of their advertising efforts.
- Our product/service is perceived as a commodity.

This list could go on and on, but you get the point. The bottom line is that some companies believe that customers exist to buy whatever products or services we decide they should want and when we decide they want them. This is not a customer-focused sales strategy. A business that wants to create products or services, advertise them, and have a sales team taking orders is *focusing on itself*. This kind of business is skating on very thin ice!

A customer-focused sales strategy begins with the customer – the *right* customer – and builds everything around the needs of the customer. This company will have a process for information sharing so that every interaction with a customer flows toward a central customer insight team. The team compiles and assesses every tidbit of information and then shares it throughout the company. In this way, the business can make all decisions based on the needs of their customers. *Customer need* drives new product/service development. Information about the customers and their needs informs marketing campaigns. Gathered by sales and customer service, sales then presents the company's response back to the customer with an explanation of how it meets customer need and why it is a good value for the customer.

Why Do I Need More Sales?

Shrinking profits place businesses under great pressure. The response of many business owners is to seek more sales. The resulting initiatives typically focus on providing training and education to make the sales team more effective, to provide better management of the sales team, or to increase sales activity. These activities are certainly worthwhile, but converting prospects into customers is only one of several key profit drivers.

If the adage is true that "profit is king," it makes sense to examine other factors affecting profitability. It is important, therefore, to expand your analysis and consider other ways to improve profitability.

Many factors affect business success and define the context in which the sales team's efforts occur. These factors might include:

- Corporate growth strategy
- Failure to understand the right customer for the business
- Quality of sales leads
- Lead nurturing process
- Customer retention strategies

Foreword   BEYOND SALES

- Sales and marketing budgets
- Failure to qualify new customers
- Inadequate systems support
- Hiring the wrong people
- Failure to manage growth

Like every other part of the business, sales success begins with the leadership team. Your corporate growth strategy must provide the goals, resources and insight needed by the sales team. Furthermore, company leaders must establish a corporate vision and maintain a unified approach throughout the organization dedicated to achieving the vision.

The sales team cannot be successful without company-wide sharing of vital information about products and services, as well as customer needs. The team needs a clear customer acquisition strategy and the training and support necessary to sell the company's products and services to the customers. Finally, the sales team needs guidance from the finance, accounting, and operations departments about the rate of growth the company can sustain at any given time.

Successful businesses understand the intricate internal relationships between all departments or teams. Rather than making any department or team the scapegoat for the company's ills, leaders need to look at the complete picture of the company.

Our Point of View

Trilogy Partners is committed to bringing multiple perspectives to analyze business strategies and achieve operational success. In this white paper, we offer a multi-perspective look at some key elements of sales strategy and success. While we do not intend to provide a primer on corporate sales, we attempt to address from our unique perspective some of the major strategic planning and implementation issues we encounter in businesses that turn to us for assistance. We also offer insights on development of corporate sales strategy and aspects of planning successfully for business growth. We conclude with a very helpful review of the critical understanding of financial reports that will help our readers manage growth while maintaining sufficient cash flow for good business health.

We hope this book will help you take a fresh look at your sales strategy. If you believe you need additional help, we hope you will read our company profile (in the back of this document). Call us if you believe our rounded approach to business management can help your organization.

Doug Brown
John Sheridan
David Wolfskehl
Hal Levenson, Founding Partner
Trilogy Partners, LLC

INTRODUCTION

INTRODUCTION

ALL BUSINESS LEADERS know their success requires sales. They know they need new customers. But from this point forward, for many companies the waters become muddied. Here are just a few of the issues that can make strategic planning a challenge:

- Making new sales is costly and time-intensive.

- Understanding customers and prospects is difficult. Assessing customer needs is challenging. Identifying the right customer is a complex process. Differences of opinion surround lead ranking.

- Many businesses believe a sale is a sale and a customer is a customer. They do not understand right and wrong customers.

- Keeping clients is important. How can a small company keep existing clients happy and recruit new customers at the same time?

- Some companies believe they are operating or producing at or near capacity. They wonder why they need more sales or new customers.

- Some businesses believe they can create a product, advertise it to the public, and count on customers storming their websites.

- Few small businesses are willing to consider controlled growth. Leaders insist they started their companies in order to grow and succeed. They are unaware of the other side of that coin.

- Many companies price products and services based on a mark up on cost. They do not ask value questions. They know they have a good product/service. If people want it, they will pay the asking price.

Is Sales the Real Problem?

If asked, "What do you need to make your business successful?" the average business owner today would likely say, "Sales." If asked,

"What would it take to make your business strong and well-positioned for the future?" the answer would likely be the same. The answer would be consistent across companies of all sizes and all industries and professions. Thousands of sales consultants agree.

Many companies need to strengthen their sales tactics or personnel. An equal (or greater) number need more than the same kind of sales to the same kind of customer, however. Their problem is not sales tactics or sales personnel. Their problem is trying to sell to the wrong people. As a result, they are not making sales or they are making sales to the wrong customers.

Before you decide your company simply needs more sales, you might do well to look deeper into the real needs of your business. You might need to ask different questions. Sales might not be your real problem.

For many companies, the problem is the type of prospects your sales team is targeting. For example, let's say you are a partner in a staffing firm. There are two other staffing firms in town. One of these firms does little in IT staffing. Your competitor has one person who does work with IT security staffing, but has significantly less experience. You have two experts in security for IT systems.

Your firm decides to focus your marketing on start-ups and small businesses. The logic involved is that these new businesses will need IT staff. But a major consideration your firm overlooked is financial: most start-ups and small businesses cannot afford the high salary necessary to have a dedicated IT security expert on staff.

Meanwhile, several companies have recently relocated to your region. Your competitor decides to target the companies relocating to the area. Their logic is that these larger companies recognize the need for an IT security specialist, can pay the salaries, and might be losing the person in this position because of the move.

Your sales team is extremely frustrated because they have won no new customers in three months. Your competitor is thriving. Their firm has brought in eight new clients who need a security expert on staff. These clients also have other IT staffing needs. The competitor is now trying to hire away your IT security experts. Although your competitor has less experience, they are winning because they targeted the right customers.

We Just Need More Sales Leads

When the sales team cannot close deals, a common response is to conclude that the marketing team is failing to produce an adequate number of solid leads. We often define "lead generation" as converting "suspects" (people who know nothing about your business) into "prospects" (people who have inquired about your business). Typically, creating leads is a marketing function.

Many business leaders leap to the conclusion that they need more sales leads. Until the current sales leads are analyzed and evaluated, however, this assessment might be faulty. The truth is if you want to improve something, you must first measure it.

There is much to measure regarding lead generation. First, your company must record the number of leads for new prospects reaching the business each day. Second, you need to know the source of each of the leads – how did each of your sales leads learn about your company? Which marketing campaigns produced the leads? Which referral source sends you the best leads? This information comes from testing and measurement.

The next step is to rank the quality of your leads by source. Which sources provide the leads that become your best customers?

A campaign or referral source generating large numbers of prospects might or might not be a good thing. For example, it is not desirable to attract price-sensitive shoppers who will spend less than your average customer spends, if they convert at all. Some marketing campaigns produce large numbers of prospects who will never become customers for one reason or another. This approach to lead generation can become quite expensive very quickly. If your efforts produce only poor quality leads, you are wasting time and money. You might also create a morale problem.

Until you take the time to analyze your leads and lead sources, you are spending money better spent on other activities. On the other hand, a well-conceived and targeted campaign might cost less and target a smaller number of prospects. If it produces an equal number of qualified leads, it is cost effective.

Consider two darts players. One stands facing away from the board and throws all three darts over his shoulder at once. One misses the board completely. The other two land between the two rings. The total score is ten points.

The other player throws each dart separately after taking careful aim. After each throw, the player reviews the throw and the position of the dart in the board. The first dart scores 15 points, but the second and third darts are in the center ring. Her total score is 65 points.

Which player would you rather be?

In the pages that follow, we will provide insights and perspectives on customers, planning sales growth, creating successful sales and growth strategies and planning for growth. Finally, we offer some insights to help you monitor your company's growth to avoid growing too fast and running out of cash.

DO I HAVE THE *RIGHT* CUSTOMERS?

☉☉☉

DO I HAVE THE *RIGHT* CUSTOMERS?

THE ONLY QUESTION some businesses ask about clients is, "Do we have *enough* customers?" This is certainly an important question. But every business should also ask other equally important questions. These include:

1. Who is the right customer?
2. Does my value proposition fit my right customer?
3. Who are my actual customers?
4. Can I fire my wrong customers?
5. Have I planned to grow my business with the right customers?
6. Do I have the resources to add new customers?
7. Do I really need new customers?
8. Are we listening to the right customers?

Who Is the *Right* Customer for Our Business?

If your company is typical, your best customers buy multiple products or services, let you know what they need from you, rank among the customers who spend the most with you, and are loyal to you. In most businesses, there are also customers who are more trouble than they are worth. Typically, the majority of your customers are ranked somewhere between the two extremes.

Your sales or customer service teams can probably tell you without hesitation who the worst customers are. They can also immediately identify your best customers. Do you know why your team ranks them in this way?

Every business needs to analyze its customer base periodically. You need to review your client book or customer list. Who are your best customers? What criteria do you use to make that determination?

- Are they your most loyal customers?
- Are they the most profitable?
- Do you have the product mix, expertise, skill to serve them?
- Do you and your team enjoy working with them?
- Are they your best referral sources?

Every business and every product/service has a *right* customer. This is the individual who:

- Has the greatest need for the benefits of the product or service provided by a firm.
- Can afford the product or service.
- Will have a long-term need for other products or services available from your company.
- Has a network of associates who might also be interested in your products or services.

☺☺☺

Does My Value Proposition Fit My *Right* Customer?

What is your value proposition? What value do you promise to your customers in exchange for the price they will pay you for products or services?

Technically, value means, "The amount of money or relative worth that is considered to be the fair equivalent for what is to be received in return." How does your company explain the value offered to customers? More important is the question, "How does your *customer* define the value you offer?"

Value is in the eye of the *buyer*, not the seller. What you think has value might not have relevant value to the buyer. We see a difference when a company believes they have a value proposition that matters to the buyer, but in the end, it is not enough. What your customer values and what they are willing to pay for it are often at odds. Do not get caught in the fallacy that what you are providing, at the cost you are providing it, is a value to your customer.

The next question to ask is, "Which customers does my value proposition fit?" If your value proposition fits the smallest spenders among your clients and your right customer is the highest spender, your value proposition needs revision. Your right customer might actually be someone who comes to you for a single product or service, but needs additional services you can provide. The point is that you must know how your customers define the value of what you provide to them. If you do not know how they define value, it is probably time to survey your customers and revise your value proposition accordingly.

Who Are My Actual Customers?

Chances are very good that many of your current customers are not your right customers. If you cannot answer the question, "Who are my actual customers?" you need to conduct a "customer audit." Gather your team and classify each of your clients based on the criteria you used to define your right customer.

One way to rank your customers is to use a five-point scale. Rank your customers this way:

1. Right
2. Likely to become right
3. Could shift in either direction
4. Likely to become undesirable customers
5. Undesirable customers

Until you know your customers, and rank them in some consistent and systematic way, you do not know how to manage their accounts. Some current customers (those you decided are more trouble than they are worth) may not be profitable for your company. Then you will need to evaluate the customers you ranked "likely to become undesirable customers" in light of your new value proposition and their response to it. If they are likely to respond negatively to price increases, they might not be worth your time and trouble.

ෛෛෛ

Can I "Fire" My Wrong Customers?

You not only can fire wrong customers, you *should* fire them. If you shift your company's focus to right customers and those who can become right, you spend your time and energy with people who are likely to want or need additional services/products from you. Imagine for a few moments what your financial reports would look like if everybody in the company focused on maximizing sales to the right customers and increasing the service levels to those who can become right customers!

You need to prepare your team to fire wrong customers. Fire these clients tactfully and honestly. You need to establish scripts or talking points to help team members plan the conversations and avoid inappropriate comments or statements. The best approach is to explain that your company decided to make strategic changes to grow the business. In light of these changes, other companies are in a better position to serve the needs of the client. Provide several recommendations of companies offering better selection, better pricing or better service for their needs. You might want to handle the "firing" in a way that still leaves a door open for the client/customer to return if the customer's needs change. Price increases can be one way to accomplish this.

ෛෛෛ

Have I Planned to Grow My Business with the Right Customers?

Your business needs a written plan for winning the right customers in order to stay on course. Your plan should also manage your rate of growth in a way that protects company profitability. What is your written plan to obtain new high-quality customers?

Your plan should be very specific about:

- Clearly defining goals.
- Identifying obstacles and solutions to overcome them.
- Action steps and schedules for achieving each of your goals.
- A clear definition of the right customers.
- Clear ideas about how and where to find your right customers.
- A clear understanding of the best way to communicate with your right customers.
- A process for qualifying new potential customers.

Without assigned responsibilities and accountabilities for your planned growth strategy, you are not likely to achieve great success. You need to be specific in assigning responsibilities and diligent in holding people accountable for their assignments. This is the only way to succeed in implementing your plan. A final check of your plan should ask:

- Is it clear?
- Is it actionable?
- Are goals achievable?
- Are the right people involved?
- Are responsibilities clear?
- Is there a defined accountability structure and process?

Do I Have the Resources to Add New Customers?

Businesses win new clients because their value proposition is attractive to the customer while also providing the company the desired or needed benefits. You must be certain you can deliver on that value proposition *before* you make the sale.

If you add new customers, you must have the staff to handle their needs and the inventory to deliver product. You must have the capital to provide additional products or services they need. Do you have adequate cash flow to survive adding new clients?

What would your company look like if you added twenty percent more new clients? Could you still provide the current level of service to existing clients? Do you have the human, inventory, systems and capital capacity to handle this increase in sales and customer need? Do you have a process for firing your bad customers to create the capacity to meet the needs of your best customers and add new high-quality customers? Do you have the right people on your team to help you make this happen?

Do I Really Need New Customers?

According to the *Harvard Business Review*, sixty-seven percent of customers who choose a new supplier say they were satisfied with their former supplier! On average, U.S. companies lose half their customer base every five years. Why do satisfied customers stop doing business with a company? The answer is that customers *go where they are wanted and stay where they are appreciated.*

Varying estimates place the cost of acquiring new customers six to ten times more than selling to existing customers. Losing customers can drastically affect your company's reputation, credibility, referrals, sales, and profitability.

Analysis of your current customer base will likely provide opportunities to sell more expensive products or services and new products and services to current customers. Many of the clients you classified as "likely to become right" will want or need additional products or services from you. Before you begin sales/marketing initiatives to win new customers, you should devote time and energy to increasing the amount your existing clients spend with you.

Are You Listening to the Right Customers?

Finally, analyze your client feedback. What is the source of the feedback? Are you listening to the right customers? Many companies discover that the largest amount of feedback and the highest intensity feedback comes from the worst clients.

You certainly do not want to build the future of your company on the feedback of the clients you plan to fire. Instead, you need to focus on the feedback of your best customers to discover what they like about your company and your team.

Next, listen to the group of clients who are most likely to become right customers. What do they like? What do they need? What will it take to make them right customers?

Finally, listen to the group in the middle. What can you learn from them about ways you need to improve? What are their needs? Can you meet those needs? Do you already offer the services or products they need – in other words, do you need to improve sales or marketing?

Before you move forward and plan your sales strategy, ensure you are listening to the right customers. Do not allow the static to overwhelm your team.

With the insights you gain from your customer base analysis, you should be prepared to think about the best and most appropriate sales and growth strategies to help your company win the right customers.

CHOOSING THE BEST SALES AND GROWTH STRATEGIES

◎◎◎

CHOOSING THE BEST SALES AND GROWTH STRATEGIES

EINSTEIN SAID THAT INSANITY is continually doing the same thing and expecting a different outcome. Many businesses fit this definition. They are stuck in a rut, doing the same thing to get customers without understanding why their efforts are a bit off target.

Every business needs a growth strategy to manage the rate of growth and to evaluate the potential of new customers before they are accepted. In this way, you protect the financial viability of your company and you ensure that you accept only the right new customers.

Many businesses, especially small businesses, become mired in misunderstandings about their customers and the needs of those customers. Many companies fail to account for the added cost of winning new customers and fail to increase the amount spent by clients.

For companies stuck in a rut, adding services or products often seems too much of a gamble. The idea of specializing is often inconceivable.

Not every growth strategy is right for every business. As the leader of your company, you must work with your leadership team (or on your own) to determine the strategy that is the best fit for your company and offers the greatest likelihood of achieving your goals and vision for the business. Then you must choose the sales strategies that will enable your team to achieve the results you desire.

Several sales strategies are available to your company to achieve your growth goals. You should understand each of the major strategies, their risks and benefits, and their fit with your goals. You might choose to implement one strategy or a combination of strategies.

◎◎◎

Client Retention

Current customers are the lifeblood of every business. *Client retention is a vital business strategy.* Without question, loyal customers are the best customers. Are your right customers truly loyal – or just temporarily satisfied?

Are you serving your existing customers to the fullest? During your customer base analysis, did you analyze existing clients to determine if they are your advocates? Are your customers satisfied with the products and service you offer them? How much higher would your profits be if you only had loyal customers? How much better would your cash flow be if you only had loyal customers? How many more services would you be providing at a higher price if you had only loyal customers? Are all of your right customers loyal? Could you grow your business faster and more economically if you only had loyal customers? Do you have a loyal customer program to ensure you only deal with loyal customers? If not, what is it costing your company? Are there enough people like your loyal customers within your realm of influence to make it likely that you can build a business on them?

You must begin by defining a "loyal customer." Your definition will likely include characteristics including:

- Willingness to tell others about you.
- Potential need for additional services or products you provide.
- A level of satisfaction with your service and relationship.
- Likelihood of remaining a customer.

Client retention tactics include:

1. Never assume you know what customers want. Ask them! Customer surveys are a good tool for understanding customer needs and identifying innovative ways to solve their problems or exceed their expectations.
2. Measure and reward customer satisfaction. If customer satisfaction is a priority in your business, demonstrate this to your team. Develop a method to measure it, set goals for improvement, and reward the team when the goal is accomplished.
3. When you hire people to interact with your customers, make sure they possess good customer services skills such as trust,

empathy, flexibility, and verbal communication proficiency. Each customer contact with your team is an opportunity to build your reputation or destroy it.

4. Say "thank you." This seems obvious. However, ask yourself when was the last time you received a thank-you note from a company with which you do business? This practice can make a very big impact and it says a great deal about your company and the value you place on customers.

5. Maintain connection with your customers by phone, mail or email. Although you might contact some clients more often, some customers should receive a "touch" quarterly.

6. Make existing valuable customers feel more appreciated than new customers or prospects. Although new customers are critical to growth, it is important for current customers to receive some VIP treatment. Programs, offers or specials exclusively for current customers will generally work well.

7. Look for opportunities to sell multiple products or services to your existing customers to create the perception of a one-stop solution provider. Research shows this builds loyalty and retention. It is also a great way to increase revenue and profit.

8. Make customer service everyone's responsibility, especially in a small business where team members wear many hats. Train your team in customer service. From the receptionist to the delivery driver, every member of your team will make an impression. The kind of impression they make is for you to determine.

Increasing Customer Spend

If you know and understand the needs of your best and most loyal customers, and you want to keep those customers, you will also want to increase "customer spend" with your firm. You can make this happen in one of two ways:

1. Sell more expensive products or services.
2. Sell additional products or services.

If you understand the needs of your best customers, your new product/service development efforts should focus on meeting those needs. As your knowledge of customer needs improves, you will also be able to anticipate customer needs and proactively develop new products and services to meet those emerging needs.

One way to help customers spend more is to *suggest the most expensive item first*. Customers are often convinced to buy the more expensive item if you immediately communicate its benefits. Never assume your customers want the cheaper product. If they cannot afford the more expensive product/service, you still have the option to sell the lower-priced item.

Helpful hints on driving your customer's attention to more expensive items include:

- Never leave it to chance. Tell every customer about the best and most expensive product or service.
- Never focus on the price. Always relentlessly sell the benefits.
- Never become pushy. Some people might be on a very tight budget. You do not want to lose the sale completely.

Another way to help customers spend more is to *stop discounting*. This means your sales will return the highest possible profit margins. If your customers shop around a lot, you might want to offer some additional incentives, such as free delivery, to help you close the sale. It is important to educate your customers on the value of doing business with you.

Helpful hints on ending discounts include:

- Focus on the *benefits* and the *quality* of your product/service; not the price.
- Offer *extra services* such as special delivery or a payment plan.
- Put aside your fear of losing the sale.

Another way to help clients spend more with you is to *add value*. Buyers assume the product at the stated price offers value. What they actually want is something that adds value. Buyers come to the table assuming that the price they pay for something will be a "fair equivalent" for what they receive. They want a good value. Regardless of the price point, buyers want to know that what they are buying is worth more than the price they pay. In other words, every customer wants to know s/he is getting a good deal.

As you define your value proposition, look for things you can offer that add exclusive, yet relevant value, but are included in your price. Then make the value-added additions a tangible part of your sales/marketing messaging. As you develop your "value pitch," remember two things: the value must be *relevant to the buyer* and it must include an *exclusive* (only you offer it) *value*. For example, a manufacturer might add free shipping on large orders. A PR firm might offer a free press release to clients who sign a one-year contract. You might offer these added values only on deluxe models or on premium packages to entice customers to spend more.

Useful tips for adding value to a deal include:

- Look for ways to add "perceived value" without increasing your cost.
- The "extras" should be part of the sales script.
- The more expensive the product, the more you offer.

Remember that you are giving away perceived value. Give away the value of an item, not its hard cost to you. If you select the bonus carefully, it will seem to be of great value to the customer; but it will cost you very little to provide.

Adding Products/Services to Meet Client Need

When you take the time to listen to client/customer needs, you are in a position to provide the additional services/products to meet those needs. In today's market conditions, it makes no sense to try to do business in the field of dreams. Producing a product or offering a service is no guarantee customers will come to you to buy.

Listening to your customers and knowing their needs should be your roadmap to the future of your business. You should produce only those products and offer only those services that meet a clear customer need. This approach reduces financial risk for your business. You will not tie up valuable resources producing and storing product you cannot sell.

Your knowledge of your best customers might reveal a desire/need to have certain services available in connection with the products or services you offer. Thus, a company that sells equipment and supplies is likely to sell more products if they provide full-service delivery, maintenance, and training to the end user. For example, a medical supply company provides various machines and supplies to patients with breathing conditions. They have invested in training several of their employees and purchasing the testing equipment used by most doctors in the area. The doctor can order the tests, evaluate patient need, and prescribe the appropriate treatment, and the company delivers it to the patient's home. In addition to delivering the machine, the staff teaches the patient to use and care for the machine, including how often to clean and change supplies. The company also makes a follow-up call to the patient each month to verify supplies needed for the next thirty days. They then ship or deliver the supplies and bill the patient's insurance company.

Small Firms Can Compete with Large Firms and Win!

Small firms can compete successfully against big firms by sidestepping a direct competition in which they cannot hope to win. Small firms can win by setting themselves apart from the crowd of their competitors by building micro-niches or by creating boutique businesses within their firms. The point is to create some unique niche or micro-niche business against which your competitors cannot compete.

By stepping outside the usual range of competition, by changing the nature of the competition and by competing based on your unique strengths, your small firm can win the new clients you need with your new micro-niche. By listening to your clients, you can identify their pain points. With some creativity and imagination, you can develop innovative responses to alleviate or remove the pain. Then you can charge premium prices for boutique products and services while cross-selling and up-selling other products.

ⓐⓐⓐ

Growth Through Niche and Micro-Niche Building

There are three excellent reasons for building a niche for your firm.

1. ***If you are perceived as an expert, you can charge premium pricing.*** Experts in every field of knowledge, every line of work, and every type of sales garner higher fees, prices or salaries because of their expertise. They are presumed to possess some inside knowledge or to have access to the movers and shakers of the industry. Making more money with less effort is an ideal way to improve your profit margins. Focusing your inventory in a specific area allows you to offer more product depth to meet customer needs
2. ***If you are an expert – if you have built a micro-niche – business will come to you.*** This alone is a great reason to become an expert serving a specific niche. You can reduce the amount of time and money you must invest in sales and marketing. The word gets around quickly in the industry or sector when you are recognized as an expert. The years of cold calls to try to drum up business will be over. Wouldn't it be nice to have clients come to your door instead of knocking on *their* door?
3. ***If you are an expert, you can differentiate yourself in the market.*** Whether you are an accountant or an attorney, a clothing retailer or a hardware distributor, you are almost certainly not the only game in town. You compete with other businesses or firms every day. Building a niche and becoming a recognized expert will

set you apart from the competition. Instead of being lost in the crowd, you will stand head-and-shoulders above the crowd.

The struggle for many professional services firms and for many product sales companies is the perceived competition between various options for the niche you will try to develop. There is much to be said for an approach that chooses the niche to focus on by just deciding that you like a particular industry, product line or type of work best.

The world tells you what you do best. If you have a ten-year-old firm, a better way to decide where to build a niche might be to look at your book of business or your customer list and see where there is a large cluster of clients. Then you carve out your niche by building upon what the world has already recognized in you.

Having determined your niche, you are then ready to start doing the work that will enable you to do the carving. Here are the steps in growing any niche.

1. **Identify how big the niche is.** How big is the industry? How much is it growing or declining? Is your customer segment a growing or declining population in your location?
2. **Identify how much of the niche you can hope to own.** How many businesses in the sector are located near you? How many of those businesses can you hope to bring into your firm? Can you do business with others in the niche outside your city? How many can you reasonably expect to make your clients? How many other stores offer a product line in your niche? Can they offer the same depth of product/ variety? Can they design their store with a single customer demographic in mind?
3. **Conduct a SWOT analysis of the competition.** How many competitors are there? What are the strengths, weaknesses and opportunities of each? How does your firm compare to the competition? What competitor weaknesses can you capitalize on to grow your place in the niche? What tactics will be necessary to do so?
4. **Plan your messaging and your marketing.** It is important to start with the message. Clarify what you want to say before you start

down the road of how to get the message out. To some degree, the message determines the medium. How will you define or characterize your firm and your expertise over and against your competitors? Then determine how you will spread the word.
5. **Grow your niche.** Get busy, get out there and get the clients. If you accomplish each of the first four steps, you will have everything you need to build your niche.

◎◎◎

Principles of Micro-Niche Building

1. If there is no customer need, there is no need for the business.
2. *Innovation* is a new response to client needs that opens new and focused opportunity.
3. Many customer needs are "pain points." These conditions cause frustration or pain. For example, a customer pain might be the time they must wait to realize the benefits of a service you provide. A customer pain might be that they do not like the limited product selection for a particular demographic.
4. Developing an innovative service, delivery method, etc. in response to customer pain creates higher customer value. Customers will pay more for high value products and services.
5. Creating unique or distinctive capabilities (like a boutique business within your firm) will draw clients who need those distinctive capabilities. The more difficult it is for your competitors to replicate the knowledge or experience that enables the new capability, the more specialized clients you will win. If your business is a retail store, your difference might be your knowledge of changing fads or trends for a specific demographic because of your expert knowledge of the customer's desires.
6. Clients will pay premium prices for innovative solutions that meet their needs – eliminate their pain – and are not available elsewhere.

Building a successful and profitable micro-niche boutique in your business depends upon your ability to build a business around the expertise of a member of the firm or the interests/needs of a specific demographic.

The market might be telling you what your firm does particularly well. You might quickly identify the experts in these high-demand areas. You might also discover that one or more of your staff would like to cultivate expertise and build a boutique business in an area that would draw in new highly profitable clients. To which partners or staff should you look for the leadership and expertise that can be the basis for a micro-niche boutique?

Who are the right people in your firm to be your experts or the leaders of the micro-niche boutiques you will build? The four main categories of potential micro-niche experts are:

1. Partners looking to re-energize a successful book
2. Technical partners
3. New partners/directors/principals
4. A partner of the future

Each of the people listed offers a unique opportunity to expand the services offered by your firm, as well as creating a practice area that will draw new clients and sell additional services to both new and current clients. As you should have learned from the process of creating and marketing practice niches, your micro-niche boutique will breathe new life into the firm and create new opportunities to grow your business strategically.

Many firms can use development of a micro-niche boutique to re-energize a successful book. Typically, any successful book will include some predominance of a particular type of work. This might be a specific service provided to a particular class of clients. It might be a group of services provided to clients in a particular industry. Opportunity to focus more narrowly within that area can be very energizing for many people. Adding a micro-niche specialty related to the currently successful book can often energize both the book and the individual.

Technical partners are those who have valuable skills in an area related to the firm's business that could become a new product or service needed by a number of the firm's clients. Unfortunately, these partners typically cannot bring in business, so they really are not maximizing their upside. A micro-niche boutique will allow them not only to bring in business, but also to bring in premium business.

New partners, directors and/or principals bring to the firm opportunity to capitalize on their previous experience and expertise. They might bring with them a developing book containing the foundation of a niche business. New partners, as their book indicates, have probably demonstrated some rainmaking ability. If they have begun to develop a specialty, a micro-niche boutique offers the opportunity to develop further both rainmaking skill and expertise in a micro-niche area. By partnering this person with a strong technical person who has the management and customer service skills needed, a strong boutique business could emerge.

When you understand some of the leading growth strategies, you can begin selecting the sales approaches that best fit your business. These will come together when you develop your company's strategic growth plan. The plan will have several components.

PLANNING FOR GROWTH

PLANNING FOR GROWTH

WITH AN UNDERSTANDING of who your best customers are and what they need from your company, and with an understanding of sales and growth strategies, you are ready to create a growth plan. It should state your vision for the future of the company, the goals you must achieve to make the vision reality and the steps you will take to make everything happen.

Your plan will describe your right customers and your definition of customer loyalty. It will outline any limits you decide to set on your future rate of growth and your plans to fire unprofitable clients.

Two additional considerations should be part of your plan as well.

Customer Selection Process

You have identified your wrong customers. Because of the cost to your company in terms of time, focus, cash and motivation, you have decided to fire these customers. Your next step is to create a customer selection process to ensure acceptance of no more of the wrong customers.

Every business needs a customer acceptance process. This is a formal process and procedure to decide which prospective clients you will accept. Your criteria for acceptance will include at least some of the following determinations:

- Likelihood of becoming high-quality customers.
- Expected profitability.
- Likelihood of needing additional products or services in the future.

Many companies establish thresholds for customer consideration. These thresholds often include

- Company size or annual income.
- Anticipated annual billing by your company.

- Type of client or business.
- Number of services needed immediately.

ⓐⓐⓐ

Customer Acquisition Process

Now that you know who your right customer is, you should have a clear process for finding and selling your company to that customer. Your process should include several critical components:

- The best salespeople within your organization.
- Key sales messages.
- Your value proposition.
- Identified centers of influence.
- Growth strategies.
- Ideal growth rate.
- Customer selection/acceptance criteria.
- Process for bringing in new clients, including listening to the needs of the customer.

Three critical policies and processes should be part of every company's sales culture: cross selling, up selling, and referral programs. Your plan should capitalize on all opportunities with existing customers and with new customers.

ⓐⓐⓐ

Plan Components

Every growth plan should include some of the following components.

1. Vision for the future of the company and goals you must achieve to create the vision.
2. Goals for growth based on an ideal rate of growth.

3. Refined Value Proposition.
4. A description of your right customers and definition of customer loyalty.
5. Plan to fire unprofitable customers.
6. Strategies and processes for retaining current customers, customer acquisition and selection, increasing customer spend and assessing customer needs.
7. Plans and processes for putting the *right* people, processes and systems in place to support your sales activities and to train and develop your team and build a sales culture.
8. Processes for building niches and micro-niches, adding services to meet customer needs and developing experts and creation of an oversight team and process.
9. A schedule for implementation and evaluation of your efforts.

It is vital to include in your growth plan an implementation schedule, an oversight process and team, and plans for evaluation of the success of your plan. Plans typically need revision and refinement. You will likely set periodic evaluations of each process and set of criteria to ensure optimal success.

Leveraging your plan to build a strong and forward-looking business in the future should be a responsibility shared by your entire team. All communication with customers should carry a consistent message. All customer interaction should communicate appreciation of the customer and should be attentive to information about emerging or unmet customer needs.

With a strategic approach to growth planning, you can position your sales team to achieve your sales goals and build the perception of the strength of your company in your marketplace. The kind of multi-faceted and multi-perspective approach outlined within these pages will maximize your success.

ABOUT THE AUTHORS

ABOUT THE AUTHORS

Douglas S. Brown, CAIA, CBC, CDIA, CVIA

In addition to being one of the founding partners of Trilogy, Doug founded Paradigm Associates LLC in 1985, and is now represented by professionals in ten states.

He is a columnist for *American Executive* magazine, has appeared on television and radio, and is a speaker at national and international conferences. His clients are business executives and sales professionals throughout North and South America, Europe, and South Africa. They span over fifty different industries and cross all sectors. In addition to his work on strategic planning issues, he is known around the U.S. as "The Sales Doctor" for his ability to diagnose missing elements of the sales process.

A believer in continuous improvement, Doug has received Certifications as a Business Coach, Total Quality Institute (TQI) Facilitator, and Analyst for the Attribute, DISC, and Values Indexes. He holds a B.A. degree in Political Science.

ⓠⓠⓠ

John Sheridan

With more than twenty-five years of business experience in companies both large and small, John brings a wealth of practical knowledge along with a passion for the game of business.

John has coached successful business owners to grow profits, build great teams, and create lasting value in a variety of industries including professional services, software and technology, manufacturing, construction, and distribution. He has earned a reputation for being direct, candid, and persistent in holding his clients accountable to defining and reaching their goals. A graduate of Boston College School of Management, John began his career in direct sales and marketing as a commercial/industrial real estate broker. That led him to a career in construction and real estate development leading profitable, growing businesses ranging in size from startups to public company business units with over one hundred million dollars in revenue.

His professional experience includes strategic planning and execution, increasing sales, improving lead generation, systematic marketing techniques, effective financial management, developing great managers and leaders, acquisitions and dispositions, business process improvement and systemization, low-risk hiring techniques, cultural transformation, improving customer service experiences, goal setting and self-mastery. Building great people who build great companies is what gives purpose to his coaching.

@@@

David Wolfskehl

David has been an entrepreneur and a guide for entrepreneurs throughout his adult life. After graduation from the University of Arizona, David founded A Bridgewater Copy and Print. Remaining within the printing industry for the next seventeen years, David next started In A Bind, and merged his operation with Action Fast Print. According to NJBIZ, Action Fast Print became the second largest quick printer in New Jersey for 2002 -2004.

David is the director of exit planning for Trilogy Partners. His focus is on helping business owners maximize the value of their greatest asset – their business. Eighty percent of small business owners have no succession plan. They are putting their families at risk and they are not maximizing the value of their businesses. Trilogy Partners exit planning group was formed to protect these families and to help the business owners.

David believes passionately in the importance of entrepreneurs interacting. To facilitate such interaction, he fulfills the following roles:

- Three-year board member of the **Entrepreneur Organization**, currently serving as its president.

- Chair of the CEO roundtable for the **Somerset County Business Partnership**.
- Entrepreneur in residence for **IFEL**, an idea incubator located on the NJIT campus, which not only helps budding entrepreneurs, but also works in economic development in urban areas.

David has received several business awards, including:

- ARC Employer of the Year.
- *Fortune Small Business Magazine* **Boss of the Year** finalist.

Hal Levenson, Founding Partner

Hal Levenson is the founder of Trilogy Partners, LLC, where he utilizes his expertise in partnering with his clients to create a realized transformation for them personally, as well as for their business. His unique skills will help clients build value in their business, as well as achieve financial security and peace of mind. A graduate of Indiana University of Pennsylvania, Hal started his career in public accounting over twenty five years ago. He founded Levenson & Burness in 1987 and later merged with LFL Veritas, LLC. In addition, Hal has also owned and invested in a multitude of other companies, in various industries from technical to retail. Always demonstrating a strong interest in civic and community affairs, he has been active in a number of organizations including: the Board of Directors of the Trenton Rotary Club, Pearl S. Buck International, Capital Health Systems, and Board member and co-founder of Goss & Goss Boxing Center, Inc.

With CPA licenses in New Jersey and Pennsylvania, Hal is a member of the American Institute of Certified Public Accountants (AICPA), the Pennsylvania Institute of CPA's (PICPA), and the New Jersey Society of CPA's (NJCPA). He is also a member of BEI, a nationwide exit planning consulting organization.

ABOUT TRILOGY PARTNERS, LLC

ABOUT TRILOGY PARTNERS, LLC

A FEW YEARS AGO, Dennis Quaid, Matthew Fox, and Forest Whitaker starred in a film entitled *Vantage Point*. It was a new approach to point of view in filmmaking. The story of an event was told from the vantage point of eight different people. It was an amazing demonstration of the importance of one's point of view in defining and relating an event. Throughout the film, the audience tried to determine which point of view reflected the truth about the event.

Business consultants can be somewhat like the characters in that film. Consultants tend to view businesses, business owners, CEOs, and business challenges from a point of view shaped by their unique knowledge base and skill set. As a result, it is conceivable that a corporate finance consultant, a leadership coach, a systems analyst, and a sales and marketing consultant could all evaluate the same company, identify a very similar list of symptoms and diagnose a different underlying cause of the symptoms.

The norm in business consulting tends to be the engagement of an individual consultant or coach with some specialization in one to three business functional areas. The consultant is selected based on the "vantage point" of the CEO as to the symptoms and the underlying cause of weakness, stress or challenge. The consultant researches the company, the industry and various business functions within the company. The consultant spends time talking with the CEO, the leadership team, and people throughout the organization.

Based on this research and analysis, the consultant then evaluates his or her findings and writes a report. In the report, the consultant outlines the symptoms and the root causes identified underlying those symptoms. The report then outlines some recommended solutions to the problems. The consultant submits his or her report and leaves.

This kind of scenario gave birth to Trilogy Partners. The firm was designed (and its design continues to evolve accordingly) to address five weakness of traditional business consulting apparent in the description above.

1. No single "vantage point" or point of view of any individual consultant is adequate to grasp the complete set of symptoms, causes and ramifications of a struggling business. At Trilogy Partners, we understand that *every individual's point of view has limitations.*
2. A second weakness of the traditional business-consulting model is that too often the information and insights gathered by the consultant are viewed through a specific lens, which might have a distortion-causing flaw or even a blind spot.
3. Writing and delivering a report, as is generally the approach of most business consultants, carries no plan for implementation of the recommended solutions.
4. There is no accountability structure incumbent upon the consultant or the business, too often resulting in the leaders of the company becoming frustrated and never making the recommended changes.
5. Sustainable solutions and lasting change seldom result from unbalanced evaluations or solutions because they fail to address all three of the essential components of most business problems. The intertwined components are:
   a. Entrepreneur's or CEO's personal and professional growth.
   b. The organization's stability, annuity, succession planning and management.
   c. Financial issues and independence.

Trilogy Partners was formed because as advisors and CPAs we were good about identifying problems and about showing solutions to clients. When it came to making it happen, however, we became distracted. We were not focused. Individually, we did not have all of the needed skill sets. Further, we were viewing businesses from a single point of view or from what the owners thought they wanted to accomplish. We discovered that even when we were focused and we brought together the requisite skill sets we were not coordinated in implementing ideas and we lacked the accountability structures to execute plans and create long-term solutions.

Because of several "light bulb moments," we understood that in order to meet the true needs and address the underlying challenges

BEYOND SALES About Trilogy Partners, LLC

facing CEOs and entrepreneurs, as well as the businesses they run, it would be necessary to re-vision the advisory approach from a different vantage point. The outcome is the Trilogy Partners advisory model, which evaluates success based on measurable results and is achieved through a highly structured process based upon constant process improvement, an ever-changing and expanding pool of CEO advisors, 360-degree assessments, and a set of interlocking accountabilities.

In all consulting work, the primary goal and task must be helping the client achieve what they are capable of doing and becoming. Unless we help the client achieve measurable transformative results, we believe our advisors have failed the client. Our goal, on the one hand, is the success and satisfaction of the client. However, advisors also must recognize that sometimes the clients do not realize they are not meeting their goals. At Trilogy, we further believe it is the role of the advisors to help the client see that they are not meeting their goals, help them develop actionable goals, and execute the action plans that will help them achieve business results or outcomes which will lead to their success.

◎◎◎

3967 Princeton Pike, Suite B
Princeton, NJ 08540
609.688-0426
www.gettrilogypartners.com

Made in the USA
Charleston, SC
11 November 2011